SECOND EDITION

Storybook 11

The
Owl Book

by Sue Dickson

Illustrations by Norma Portadino, Jean Hamilton, Chip Neville and Kerstin Upmeyer

Printed in the United States of America

Copyright © 1998 Sue Dickson
International Learning Systems of North America, Inc.
St. Petersburg, FL 33716

ISBN: 1-56704-521-9 (Volume 11)

C D E F G H I J K L M N—CJK—05 04 03 02 01 99

Table of Contents
Raceway Step 24

Bozo the Clown Comes to Town

Vocabulary

1. chow
2. shower
3. towel
4. town
5. now
6. down
7. brown
8. flower
9. flowers
10. cow
11. Howard

12. owl
13. wow
14. clown
15. frown
16. bow
17. bowed
18. howl
19. howled
20. gown

Story Word

21. uncle

3

Andy jumped from his bed and ran to take a shower. Then he dried with his towel and ran to get dressed.

Today was Andy's big day. The circus had come to town at last!

"Hurry down to eat," yelled Mom. "It's nine o'clock now. We must be in town by ten. Uncle Howard will meet us at the big tent."

"I like the flowers in your dress, Mom. You look pretty," Andy said.

"You look fine in your brown shirt, too, Andy," said Mom.

Andy ate his eggs.

Then Mom said, "Andy, go open the gate for Brown Cow. She can go eat grass on the hill. I will feed Lassie some dog chow. Then we will go."

When Andy came back,
he asked, "Now can we
go ? I can't wait to see
the circus !"

"Yes, now it is time to
go," said Mom.

8

Uncle Howard met Mom
and Andy at the big tent.

Andy looked way up to
the top. "Wow !" cried
Andy.

"It **is** big," said Uncle
Howard. "Now come with
me, Andy. We will go see
Bozo the Clown get dressed."

Uncle Howard and Bozo were pals.

"Hi, Andy," said Bozo. "Would you like to see me paint my face ?"

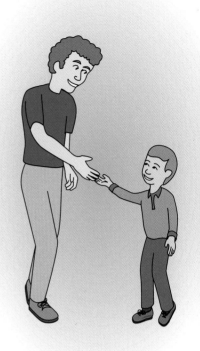

"Wow ! Yes !" said Andy.

Bozo the Clown put thick white cream on his face.

Then he painted fat red lips. Next, he put a big red spot on each cheek.

"Now what
is missing ?"
said Bozo
with a frown.

"Your big
red nose !"
said Andy.

Bozo put on his huge
red nose and bowed to
Andy. Andy just howled !

Then Bozo and Uncle Howard, Mom and Andy rushed to the big tent.

"We must not miss the first act," cried Andy.

"And I must not miss my big act," said Bozo. "I will wave to you, Andy. Have fun at the circus today."

13

Andy liked
all the clowns
best...

fat clowns,
skinny clowns,
red clowns
and brown.

One in a funny gown,
up-side down!

A clown
with an owl...

A clown
with a
flower...

16

A clown in a bath-tub
taking a shower !

A clown
that could
howl...

A clown
with a cow...

18

And best of all, Bozo, taking a bow !

The End

Vocabulary

1. house
2. scout
3. scouts
4. sound
5. sounds
6. proud
7. around
8. shout
9. shouted
10. flour
11. about
12. couch

13. scouting
14. ground
15. bounce
16. found
17. our
18. loud

<u>Story Words</u>

fin ish
finish
19. finished

pā per
20. paper
21. says (sez)

20

Joan ran into the house.
"Mommy !" she shouted.
"Look at this paper. My
teacher gave it to me. It
says that I may be a
Brownie Scout !"

"Lots of the girls in my class will be Scouts," Joan went on. "I can't wait !"

"That sounds like fun," said Mother. "We can go see the Brownie Scout leader. This paper tells me that Miss Proud will be the leader."

"She lives just around the corner," shouted Joan. "Let's go see her now!"

Mother said, "First, I need to finish this pie crust, and I must wipe the flour off my hands, Joan. Then we will go."

When Mom had finished, she and Joan went to see Miss Proud.

"We would like to find out about Brownie Scouts," said Joan.

Miss Proud said, "Come in the house. You can sit here on my couch."

Miss Proud then told Mom and Joan about Scouting. She said, "We will go on a camp-out. We will sleep on the ground in tents. Do you have a sleeping bag, Joan?"

"Yes," said Joan.
"Daddy has a sleeping
bag. He was a Scout."

Joan was so happy, she
began to bounce up and
down on the couch.

"Sit still, Joan," said
Mom. "I'm glad we found
out about Scouts. It
sounds like fun !"

"We must go now," said Mom. "It has been about an hour and I have a pie in the oven."

Joan gave a loud shout. **"YIPPEE !"** she said. "I am going to be a Brownie Scout !"

The End

The Snowman

Vocabulary

1. snow

2. snowing

snow   man
3. snowman

4. low

5. slow

6. throw

7. crow

8. row

9. grow

10. bow

11. window

12. show

13. blow

14. snowball

It was the first snow of the winter. Ted, Karen and Liz ran out to make a big snowman.

29

"The north wind doth blow, and we shall have snow ... and a snowman," said Dad. He was looking out the window at the children.

"Come see the fine show, Mother," he said.

"Look, here is a carrot
for his nose," said Ted.

"And two black coals so
he can see," said Karen.

"Let's put this bow tie
on his neck," said Liz.

Dad said, "Let's get a hat for the snowman, Mom. We can go out and help finish him."

"You will never grow up," Mom said. "Let's go ! We can throw some snowballs, too !"

"OK Mom, not so slow !" said Dad.

And out they went !

Mom put the hat on the snowman.

"Look, Dad! We put stones in a row for his buttons," said Liz.

"I'll put this pipe in his mouth," said Dad.

33

"Now **there** is a snowman to crow about !" said Dad.

"Let's go in for some hot chocolate," said Mom.

"Yes," said Dad. "We can see our snowman from the window. If it keeps on snowing, we may see him **grow !**"

The End

The New Crew

Vocabulary

1. few

2. flew

3. mew

4. threw

5. new

6. crew

7. screw

8. screws

9. stew

10. chew

Bobby and Steve lived near a pond.

"Let's make a raft to sail on the pond," said Steve.

"Yes," said Bobby. "We can get some logs at my house."

36

"I will get a hammer and nails and screws," said Steve.

"Wait," said Bobby. "I must go home to eat now. I will meet you after lunch."

"OK," said Steve.

"Don't chew the stew so fast, Bobby," said his mom. "What is the rush?"

"Steve and I are going to make a raft. We will sail it on the pond. We will be the crew," said Bobby.

"That will be fun," said Mom. "How about a few cookies and some gum to chew? I will put them in a bag for you and Steve. You can eat them as you make the raft."

"Thank you, Mom," said Bobby, and off he flew to meet Steve.

39

On his way Bobby met Willy, his big cat.

"Mew, mew," went Willy.

"Would you like to come with me, Willy?" asked Bobby. Willy rubbed Bobby's leg.

Bobby and Steve began making the raft. Hammers and nails flew!

At last the raft was finished. It even had a sail on a mast!

Just as Steve and Bobby threw the raft into the pond, a bird flew by. He flew up to sit on the mast!

All at once, lots of things

happened ! Willy jumped
onto the raft to get that
bird ! As he jumped, a
big puff of wind blew on
the sail ! The rope flew
out of Steve's hand...and
away went the raft across
the pond !

"Look at the new crew!"
yelled Bobby and Steve.
They both giggled and
giggled at such a funny
thing!

It tickled those boys.
Would it tickle you to see
this new and funny crew?

The End

Quite a Surprise

Vocabulary

1. quite

2. question

3. quilt

4. quit

5. quick

6. queen

7. quiz

qui̅ et
8. quiet

<u>Story Words</u>

do ing
9. doing

al ways
10. always

go ing
11. going

her self
12. herself

Jean was so quiet !

Mom asked, "What are you doing, Jean ? What are those little scraps of cloth ?"

Jean was sorry her mom had asked that question. She had hoped to have a surprise for her.

"I am going to make something for you," said Jean. She hoped that Mom would not quiz her more.

Then Mom gave Jean a quick look and said, "I hope it will not be a dress !"

They both giggled.

Jean was making a quilt for Mom. She would have to quit when Mom's quick steps came near.

"I must get this quilt finished on time," said Jean to herself.

On Mother's birthday,
Jean's surprise was finished.
"A quilt !" Mother cried
when she saw it. "It is so
pretty ! This is quite a
surprise. Even a queen
would love this quilt, Jean !"

"You are **my** queen,
Mom !" said Jean.

Mom gave Jean a big hug. "Thank you, Jean," she said. "I will always see your love in each little stitch of that quilt ! Thank you for a very happy birthday !"

The End

The New White Car

Vocabulary

1. white
2. which
3. where
4. when
5. wheel
6. wheels
7. wheat
8. Wheaties
9. whiz
10. what
11. whipped
12. whopper
13. while

a while
14. awhile

Story Words

15. sīgn
16. sīgns
17. who
18. car

50

The Millers have a new white car. They are going on a trip in it. Mom is going to look at the map to see which roads to take.

Dad will drive for awhile.

Sam and Frank will look at the road signs so they can tell where they are and when to turn.

"I just love this new steering wheel," said Dad.

"What is that growing
over there ?" asked Frank.

"That is wheat," said Dad.

56

Mom asked, "Who can tell me what is made from wheat ?"

"Wheaties !" yelled Frank.

"What else ?" asked Mom.

"Hamburger rolls," Dad said. "Shall we stop at the next hamburger place we see ?"

"Look at that sign," said
Sam. "I can read it.
W-H-I-Z! WHIZ INN!"

"I see it," said Frank.
"Hamburgers. Soda. Let's
whiz in there, Dad."

"It looks like a nice
place," said Mom. "Yes,
let's whiz in there."

"See their flag whipping in the wind," said Sam.

Dad drove in and stopped the car. The Miller family got out.

"When we come back out, it will be Mom's turn to drive our new car," said Dad.

"Good !" said Mom.
"That will be fun."

The End

Where is that popsicle man ?

Where is his white truck with the red wheels ?

What will you buy when he comes ?

I want a whipped cream whopper !

The End

64